When The Purple Waters Came Again

Words by Norman C. Habel
Pictures by Jim Roberts

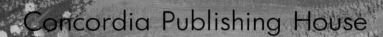

Concordia Publishing House

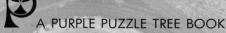

A PURPLE PUZZLE TREE BOOK
COPYRIGHT © 1971 CONCORDIA PUBLISHING HOUSE, ST. LOUIS, MISSOURI
CONCORDIA PUBLISHING HOUSE LTD., LONDON, E. C. 1
MANUFACTURED IN THE UNITED STATES OF AMERICA
ALL RIGHTS RESERVED
ISBN 0-570-06503-8

When Adam and Eve left the Garden of Eden,
the garden vanished from sight.
And nobody's seen it since.
Have you?

When Adam and Eve left the Garden of Eden,
things just weren't the same.
And nobody seemed to care.
Do you?

When Adam and Eve left the Garden of Eden,
they had two healthy sons.
And I know both their names.
Do you?

That's right.
The one was Kingpin Cain.
And the other was Nobody Abel.
Cain worked very hard
to make his wheat and barley grow.
Abel watched the goats and sheep
no matter where they'd go.

At harvest time
both Cain and Abel came to worship God.
Cain brought sacks of grain
and Abel brought some sheep,
the sweetest he could find.
When God saw both these gifts
He knew how Cain and Abel felt
about their God.

So God said, "Cain, your gift is gross.
You have a selfish heart.
Abel, your gift is good.
I love you Abel, you Nobody!
And that makes you somebody."

Well, Cain was very angry
and asked his brother Abel
to meet him in the fields.
There Cain killed his brother Abel
when he thought no one was looking.
"Now," yelled Cain, "You *are* nobody,
for you're absolutely dead."

Then the blood of Abel
that was spilled on the ground
screamed to God for help.
And God came running fast.
"Where's your brother Abel, Cain?"
said God, "I can hear him crying 'HELP'!"

"How should I know, God?" said Cain.
"Am I supposed to watch my brother
and care for him all day?
If I have to baby-sit that guy,
then, God, You have to pay."

"No, you're the one who has to pay,"
said God, like a very angry father.
"You won't pay with money
but with fear inside your heart.
For everywhere you go,
someone else will want to kill you,
because you killed your brother Abel."

"That's more than I can stand," said Cain,
   with tears inside his heart.
"I need some help from You."
   So God, who loves all men,
   gave Cain another chance.
   He placed a bright red mark on Cain
   to show all other men:
   They had no right to kill King Cain,
   for God had forgiven him.

But the days of Cain were evil days,
   and so were the years that followed.

Those were the days
   when big black dinosaurs
   with fierce roars
   and screeching snores
   would stomp
   and clomp
   and romp
   through the purple swamp.

Those were the days
   when ferocious hairy giants
   with enormous gleaming eyes
   wandered through the night like ghosts.

So when God saw
that everyone was wicked
and all the world was evil,
He said to Himself, "That's it!
I'll bring the world to an end.
I'll tear it up completely,
and I'll start all over again!"

What do you think will happen
if God tears the world in two?
Do you think He'll save some pieces
to start the world anew?

Then there came a rumbling,
Rummmble-Rummmble-Rummmbling,
like the sound of a giant
mumbling and grumbling,
trying to open a door

underneath the ground...
And suddenly,
the earth was split wide open,
and the land was covered
with water and mud galore!

Then there came a thundering,
Thun-dun Dun-dun Dun-dering,
like the sound of a giant blundering,
trying to open a door
in the ceiling up above...
And suddenly,
the heavens split open wide.
And from the sky above
more water began to pour.

The world had split in two,
and the world filled up with water,
very dirty water,
that looked a dirty purple.
The water kept on churning,
churning round and round,
and up and down
and in and out
and everywhere there was.
And it made an ugly sound,
like chuuuurple
chuuuurple chuuuurple

So God punished all the world
and everything He made,
for all the men were evil
and very, very bad!

But a very strange thing happened
in the middle of all this mess.
God saved some special pieces
from the old world He had made.
He snatched them from the purple waters,
just as we are saved
the day that we are baptized
with water and with love.

The first piece was Noah,
an old, old man called Noah,
and all his family too.
God told old man Noah to build a boat
and make a floating zoo.

So he took some ants,
and he took some snails,
some clumsy kangaroos
who have very funny tails.
He took some fish,
and he took some crows,
and some camels with a hump,
and the happy hippopotamus
who has very dirty feet
that make a funny sound,
like phump,

shluuuurphump
shluuuurphump

And he took a few
of all the things
that came up two by two,
to be the very first to live
in that great floating zoo.

For months and months
and months and months,
the world was full of water,
dirty purple water.
Then one day,
one new year's day,
the land appeared again
like a big dry hump,
a bumpy, lumpy, humpy hump,
that came between the waters
and stopped the dirty water
from churning round
and up and down
and in and out
and everywhere there was.

By the end of one long year
the world was made anew.
So Noah and his animals
left their floating zoo.

Then Noah was told,
like Adam of old,
to start all over again,
to rule for God
and rule the world
just as Adam had done.

And Noah was told
to look and behold
a rainbow high
in the stormy sky.
That rainbow is a promise
that the dirty purple waters
will never come again,
never, never, never.

And I'm sure they never will,
aren't you?

OTHER TITLES

the PURPLE PUZZLE TREE